*Id*onomics

by

Hoyt Hilsman

Id, Ego and the Pleasure Principle

In the late 1960's, at the Bing Nursery School on the campus of Stanford University, Walter Mischel, an Austrian-born research psychologist began an interesting experiment involving four-year olds and marshmallows. He offered the children a tempting choice – they could have one marshmallow right away, or if they waited a few minutes, they could have two marshmallows. Videos of the kids struggling with deferred gratification show their anxiety as they cover their eyes and fidget anxiously, trying to avoid eating the delicious treat that is right in front of them. Most of the kids couldn't hold out more than three minutes before eating the marshmallow. About thirty percent, however, were able to delay gratification for about fifteen minutes.

Mischel's experiments, along with his follow-up of his subjects over the next thirty years, spawned a whole range of studies into the mechanics and sources of delayed gratification. Mischel's findings that the thirty percent of children who were able to resist temptation had higher academic achievement and better personal relationships later in life also generated great controversy. This in turn led to studies into the psychological, neurological, genetic and cultural sources of delayed gratification. Theories sprung up in the fields of social psychology, medicine, political science, economics and even philosophy about the reasons why people might delay immediate gratification.

No matter where these studies and resulting theories led – and they were often inconclusive and uncertain – they always return to a fundamental question for human beings – do we eat the marshmallow now or later? Do we postpone immediate pleasure for some future reward? Do we embrace the pleasure principle or do we override it – either in the name of some overarching principle or simply because it will benefit us to wait?

Sigmund Freud was one of the first modern thinkers to tackle this aspect of human behavior in his structural model of the human psyche. In Freud's view, the id is a fundamental component of our personality that works to satisfy our basic urges, needs and desires. The id is critical to our survival as newborns. When a baby is hungry, it wants food and cries. When the baby is cold, or in pain, or needs attention, the id demands that his or her needs be met.

For Freud, the id was based on the pleasure principle, pure and simple. The pleasure principle says that people will seek pleasure and avoid pain in order to satisfy their biological and psychological needs. The id doesn't care about reality or the needs of others. It seeks only its own satisfaction. To the id, nothing else is important.

In Freud's model, as the child gets older, the ego develops, which is based more on the reality principle and the needs of others. Finally, the child develops the superego, which Freud believed was a result of the moral and ethical restraints placed on us by parents and other authority figures. For the healthy person, the ego acts to satisfy the needs of the id and not upset the superego, while at the same time taking the reality of each situation into consideration. If the id gets too strong, self-gratification takes over. If the superego gets too strong, a person would become rigid, moralistic and out of touch with reality.

While Freud's theories have been sliced and diced, revised, dissected and tossed out by many later critics, there remain some fundamentally important insights in his model of human psychology. Subsequent research by neuroscientists has in fact identified the pleasure centers of the brain, and their findings support the fundamental ideas of Freud. The researchers identified two essential motivations in the physiology of human behavior – appetitive and aversive. Appetitive motivation includes the desire for food, sex and other needs while aversive motivation is the desire to avoid pain. The physiological research identified separate, but related neural pathways that mediate reward and aversion. Through electrical and chemical stimulation, the researchers were able to activate these neural pathways and gain insight into the physiology of our reward systems.

This research has given us great insights into how the brain functions in pursuit of the pleasure principle; for example, in the sources and mechanics of addiction. However, it has not answered fundamental questions about how we temper our impulses in pursuit of the pleasure principle, how we consider the cost or benefit of our actions, and how we can defer immediate gratification when it may be in our best interest to do so. Studies have shown, for example, that simple "will power" or just "saying 'no'" is not enough to override our need for immediate gratification. So how do these powerful drives operate in the real world, and how do they impact our daily lives – and the future of the American Dream?

Lessons from The Great Recession

The event that has most significantly the American Dream in recent years is the Great Recession. While one could debate endlessly the roots of the Great Recession and the global financial crisis, it arguably goes back as far as the 1960's and the coming of age of the baby boomer generation. The baby boomers, growing up amidst the civil rights struggles and the Vietnam war, rebelled against the traditions of earlier generations, resisted authority and rejected tradition in their protests against racism, sexism, the military draft and a host of other issues. What they sought, in a time of unprecedented economic growth, was freedom from the strictures that their parents and grandparents had placed on them and on society in general.

In many ways, the baby boomers succeeded beyond their expectations in removing social and economic barriers for women, minorities and other disenfranchised groups, and in freeing themselves from the traditional roles of the past. They wanted a more open society, with greater freedom from traditional rules and more opportunity for all. In short, they wanted to expand the scope of the American Dream to include equal opportunities and greater freedom for everyone. And, to a large extent, they succeeded.

However, the new freedoms also brought with it greater temptations and further possibilities for abuse. The sexual revolution, while freeing women from traditional roles and giving them more choices, also opened the floodgates for sexual exploitation, commercialization of sex and disruption of traditional mores. New career opportunities for women also meant a larger, more productive workforce, but also led to a disruption of traditional family life as both husband and wife had jobs and careers.

With the 1970's and the advent of the storied "Me Generation," there was a much greater emphasis on personal fulfillment and individual development. While this offered many opportunities for exploration of the self beyond the traditional gender and social roles, it also led to a focus on the individual, sometimes at the expense of the greater community. It also undermined the ethic of self-sacrifice that had been an historic component of the American character.

In the 1980's Reagan era, the focus on individuality blossomed into fewer government restrictions on businesses and marked the beginning of the deregulation of the marketplace. While this meant greater opportunities for companies to expand without the strictures of government regulation, it also led to a more Darwinian economic environment. Traditionally, American businesses had been focused not simply on profit, but also in providing quality products and services for their customers and value for their shareholders. They generally had long-term goals that led to investments in the company's future rather than short-term profits for investors.

However, by the 1990's, with the arrival of the global marketplace, companies became more focused on their stock price, often at the expense of their long-term future, and executives were rewarded more for the increase in the company's stock price than for the growth of revenues. In addition, the global marketplace meant that companies operated outside of the regulatory reach of single countries, and global competition drove them toward a more unrestrained, bottom line approach that focused on immediate results. As the global marketplace became less restrained by regulation and more dominated by fierce competition, companies embraced greater and greater risk, often reaping huge rewards, but sometimes courting monumental failure.

More competition and less regulation also impacted average Americans. Beginning in the 1980's, deregulation meant looser credit for all Americans. While previous generations had saved for large purchases like houses, cars, appliances or vacations, easy credit meant that millions of people could buy today, and pay later with their credit cards. Less regulation, along with competition for customers, meant easier and easier credit for everyone, and mailboxes were flooded with credit offers that were very hard to refuse. At the same time, with competition building for the consumer dollar, more and more was spent on advertising and marketing to get people to buy lots of things that they didn't really need. Products and services that were luxuries that were beyond the reach of previous generations of middle-class Americans were marketed as necessities, or at least important status symbols.

The result was predictable – millions of Americans fell into debt, burdened by large credit card balances and unwieldy mortgage payments. For a long time, this didn't present a huge problem, because there were still plenty of good jobs, and, with both husband and wife working, it was still possible to keep up with the debt payments. On top of that, the stock market was booming, which helped many Americans who had 401(k) plans, and the housing market was on the upswing, so people felt wealthier.

As we all know, the endless cycle of easier credit, less regulation and booming markets fed upon itself until it all came crashing down with the Great Recession. The bubble that burst created an opposite reaction – a downward cycle that fed on itself as people lost jobs, the housing market tanked and financial markets crashed. More foreclosures and bankruptcies led to greater suffering that fed on itself. While we are beginning to climb out of the Great Recession, its impact will be felt on America and the American Dream for years to come.

Idonomics

So what is behind the cycle that began in the 1960's and resulted in the excesses of the late twentieth century and the Great Recession of the twenty-first century? Is it simply part of the ebb and flow of the worldwide economy? Or is it just human nature to fall victim to endless cycles of boom and bust? Certainly there have been periods throughout human history when economies have risen and fallen, and when human greed and risk-taking has result in great catastrophes from depressions to wars and famines. But is this period somehow different, and, if so, what is the underlying dynamic that we are experiencing?

If we go back to the marshmallow experiment, we see that only about one-third of the children in the experiment are able to defer gratification for very long in the face of temptation. While it may be to their benefit in the long term to hold out for greater rewards, most people are not able to do so, especially as they are tempted by instant gratification in the form of easy credit, low down payments or other inducements to buy now and pay later. However, that doesn't explain why earlier generations – notably the World War II generation, the so-called Greatest Generation – was markedly more conservative in their approach to indebtedness and risk in general.

For one thing, the Greatest Generation had lived through times of great economic and social upheaval, most notably the 1929 Crash, the Depression and World War II. They had witnessed real catastrophes in their lives and were therefore more conservative in their approach to risk. They put down at least twenty percent on their houses, paid off their mortgages before retiring, and fought for predictable retirement pensions and Social Security. They had seen the world descend into chaos and destruction, and so they looked for strong and conservative political leadership, as well as social rules that promoted not only freedom for the individual, but also community cooperation. "The greatest good for the greatest number" might well have been the slogan of the Greatest Generation, and while it may have socialist overtones today, it was the foundation of the New Deal, and later the Great Society, which was built by that generation to provide a social support system for all Americans, as well as provide an equal shot at the American dream.

When John Kennedy said in his inaugural address, "Ask not what your country can do for you, but rather what you can do for your country," Americans were inspired by the emphasis on patriotism and self-sacrifice. Today, any politician who uttered similar sentiments would likely be attacked from both the left and the right, either for being a socialist or for being unduly nationalistic. In the current era, the emphasis has shifted to the rights of the individual, whether it is the outcry on the right for less government and more individual freedom, or on the left for greater civil liberties and more help for the disadvantaged. The idea of individual sacrifice for the sake of the nation is simply not a priority.

For the past fifty years, since President Kennedy made that speech on a frosty January morning in 1961, Americans have retreated from self-sacrifice to individual gratification. We have gone from a healthy sense of deferred gratification to a morbid focus on instant rewards. We have traded our traditional economic and social values for "idonomics" – the pursuit of the pleasure principle. In the bargain, we have abandoned the common sense that has been a hallmark of the American character. And we have put the American Dream at risk.

Idonomics Gone Wild

It's pretty easy to see how idonomics operates in the worlds of business and the American consumer. With easy credit, looser regulations and lots of tempting offers, you can understand how executives might go after a big payday by pumping up their stock price with short-term gimmicks that ignore the longer term and even put their companies at risk. Perhaps one can sympathize with the young couple who take advantage of the no-money-down, zero-income offers to buy a house or a car. Or why a homeowner might jump at the chance to refinance her home with a cash-out deal to upgrade her kitchen or take a European vacation.

Sure, it's easy to ignore the consequences of a million individual economic decisions, even if they are more than a little bit risky. Because a million small economic risks can add up to one great big systemic risk, as we discovered during the 2008 financial meltdown that precipitated the Great Recession. While the average person may be only taking a small risk, the big players are often taking gigantic risks. The insurance giant AIG, for example, took on hundreds of billions of dollars in foolish risk, only to be bailed out by the American taxpayer, who ended up footing most of the bill.

Idonomics also creates huge opportunities for fraud, both great and small. From the commissions that mortgage brokers took from underqualified home buyers to the $60 billion that Bernie Madoff stole from his investors, idonomics was at the heart of the fraud. People simply abandoned common sense in pursuit of the pleasure principle, and we all ended up suffering as a result.

However, it is not just in the consumer and business arenas that idonomics can wreak havoc. In fact, idonomics has an impact on virtually every aspect of our lives, from politics and entertainment, to sports and religion, not to mention our health and personal relationships. The consequences of idonomics in all of these areas can be surprising, and are vast in their scope.

Political Idonomics

One would think that instant gratification would have no place in government. After all, we have inherited a thriving and prosperous democracy that is more than two hundred years old. We have fought a revolution, a bloody civil war and two world wars to preserve our freedoms. Why would we put all that at risk in pursuit of instant gratification and pleasure? In fact, that's exactly what we have been doing for more than thirty years. Beginning with the Reagan era, our federal budget deficits have skyrocketed as politicians promised voters that they could have the pleasure of generous government programs without the pain of paying for them through taxation or other revenues. You couldn't look for a better textbook example of idonomics in action.

Politicians – and ultimately the voters – on both the left and right share the blame for the idonomics idiocy. On the left, politicians promised voters benefits that everybody knew were unaffordable in the long run, and covered up the problem with accounting tricks. While on the right, politicians refused to raise taxes, closed loopholes for the wealthy and corporations, and undermined the property tax base with initiatives like Proposition 13 in California. And both the left and the right resorted to accounting tricks to hide the red ink, or relied on the occasional budget surpluses that resulted from economic bubbles to conceal the real problems.

As the government expanded its programs, cut taxes and focused on pork barrel subsidies, it ignored essential investment in infrastructure, education and other critical areas. And it wasn't just the federal government that was practicing idonomics, it was also the state and local governments, who committed themselves to unworkable pension plans and other expenditures, even as they refused to boost revenues through taxation or other sources. After thirty years of idonomics, we are seeing the result in fierce fights over governmental budget, and a citizens' revolt in the form of the Tea Party.

Another unforeseen consequence of idonomics in the political sphere is the rife partisanship in the halls of Congress and in state and municipal governments around the country. What could be a better example of idonomics than the short-term mission of members to get themselves re-elected every two years? Despite an incumbent re-election rate of over ninety-five percent, members of Congress spend the majority of their time raising millions of dollars to fund their campaigns, much of which comes from special interests and lobbyists. To make matters worse, the political parties fight viciously to gerrymander safe congressional districts for themselves, which means that most districts are either solidly Democrat or solidly Republican. That means that the real elections are the primaries, where candidates jockey to be the most liberal or most conservative. No wonder the Congress is hopelessly deadlocked, unable to compromise.

Idonomics in Health Care

When it comes to our health, it would be silly to take unnecessary risks, right? Why would we ignore the advice of our doctor to take a pill, go into the hospital or follow a treatment plan? And why would we pursue short-term fixes when we have a serious, chronic problem? That would be like taking aspirin for an appendicitis attack. And yet that's exactly what we have been doing with our heath care – both individually and as a society. We've been practicing health care idonomics instead of good medicine.

Let's look at the health care industry today. (Maybe you'd rather not, but that's another issue). Insurance companies, drug companies, hospitals and health care providers are all looking to make a profit. While there is nothing wrong with that in theory, profit-making these days is all about boosting the bottom line in the short-term. Health care corporations are like every other business – they are answerable to their shareholders, who are looking for the higher return each and every quarter on their investment. Sound familiar? It's classic idonomics.

Drug companies are a prime example. They spend millions of dollars on researching new drugs, but what are the drugs that they are spending all that money to develop? Drugs that will have the biggest potential market. So drugs used to treat illnesses that affect a smaller chunk of the population are generally ignored. Or drugs that can be used to <u>cure</u> a disease may not be as profitable as those that <u>treat</u> a disease over a long time. And what are the drugs that are the most profitable? Those that address impotence, aging, appearance and weight loss. While low libido, incontinence, wrinkled skin and extra fat are certainly not desirable, it is questionable whether a huge chunk of drug industry research should be going to treating those conditions – not to mention the huge advertising and marketing budgets that accompany the rollout of those drugs. Drugs to improve our sex lives, reverse aging and lose weight are a clearly in pursuit of the pleasure principle – and an example of idonomics gone wild.

Health insurance companies are also major practitioners of idonomics. The whole idea of health insurance was to provide a safety net against the possibility of a serious illness that could wipe out a family's finances. But health insurers now screen out anybody they suspect of potentially developing a serious illness. That turns the whole idea of insurance on its head – with only healthy people who are unlikely to get sick being protected against the possibility of illness while the rest of the population is left either uninsured or paying exorbitant premiums. Again, a case of idonomics where the real goal is quarterly share price of the company.

Government programs like Medicare and Medicaid are no exception to the rule of idonomics in health care. Instead of operating a health care system based on results, these government programs are based strictly on the quantity of health care delivered. Rather than assuming some responsibility for the overall quality of our nation's health, the government simply throws money at health care providers in the hope that they will use their resources wisely. At the same time, doctors and hospitals waste enormous amounts of money on unnecessary tests either because patients want them or because of their fear (often unfounded) of lawsuits. On top of that, government payments are standardized, so that doctors have an incentive to increase the volume of patients, thus resulting in less time with each patient and a lower quality of care.

Ultimately, health care consumers are also trapped in the web of health care idonomics. Either they have a gold-plated health care plan (fewer and fewer people have this), so that they demand expensive and unnecessary services, or they have a high deductible (or no insurance at all) and end up postponing necessary treatment and end up being treated in the emergency room (at a much higher cost). The bottom line is that the individual patient has very little control over the process and is a victim of the vicious cycle of idonomics.

In a sense, the whole health care system is a victim of idonomics. As Americans, we believe that we have the most advanced health care system in the world, with access to stunning new technologies and innovative methods for curing disease. In one way, this is absolutely true. Americans have access to some of the best medical technologies in world. But they are also very expensive. The idea that all Americans can have access to these very costly treatments without paying for them is, pure and simple, idonomics. Unless we are willing change our view of health care to balance the needs of the individual with the cost to society, our health care system is ultimately doomed. It's a case of facing reality, which idonomics strenuously avoids.

Media, Entertainment, Idonomics

Sensationalism has always been an aspect of the media world, going back to the "yellow journalism" of William Randolph Hearst and centuries before that. The media and entertainment industries are all about grabbing the attention of readers and viewers through flashy headlines, prurient images or outrageous opinionating. But there have always been two sides to the media and entertainment worlds – the cheap and gaudy side that aimed to grab our attention through sleaze and sop, and the more serious side that sought to communicate a deeper message or provide thoughtful, engaging entertainment. In an era of idonomics, you don't have to guess which side has triumphed.

Television news used to be dominated by three powerful networks – CBS, ABC and NBC. The nightly newscasts were hosted by serious, experienced journalists like Walter Cronkite, Howard K. Smith and David Brinkley, who had enormous influence over our national debates. Local TV news was something of a journalistic afterthought, reporting community events, the weather and cute animal stories. Newspapers operated in a similar way, with the powerful city newspapers dominating the national scene, while local papers in smaller cities kept readers abreast of local events. These news organizations were very profitable, with large audiences and readerships, and plenty of money rolling in from advertisers eager to grab the attention of consumers. These media outlets were viewed not simply as profitable companies, but as providing an important public service of informing the citizens of a democracy. While their public service character might have been doubtful, it was the generally prevailing view.

With the arrival of idonomics, all that changed. Owners of media companies began to see them not so much as a public trust as an opportunity to promote shareholder value. Beginning in the 1980's, there was a frenzy of merger and acquisition activity as television broadcasters, publishers and newspaper companies that might have been under family ownership for generations changed hands rapidly. Suddenly – and it was pretty sudden – media companies began to value the bottom line, specifically the quarterly bottom line, much more than before. Longtime owners sought to cash in on their legacy investments, and investors went deeply into debt as they speculated on a quick payoff.

At the same time, deregulation and new technologies changed the landscape of media and entertainment profoundly, giving consumers much greater choices about the television shows they watched, the news they read or saw on TV and the music they listened to. With the arrival of cable television in most homes, cable news stations sprung up with 24-hour coverage that undermined the traditional broadcast evening news shows. And with cable news vying for viewers' attention, news shows became more and more sensationalistic and opinionated as they sought to capture one demographic after another.

With the rollout of the internet, information itself became a commodity rather than a valued quantity. Audiences and readers began looking for easy, instant answers rather than taking the time for considered reflection on complex information. The era of bumper sticker ideology and wedge issues had begun. Again, the pursuit of easy digested, simple solutions replaced more complicated, deferred gratification -- the triumph of idonomics.

But, as fans of movies, music and television know well, it isn't just the information side of the media world that suffers from idonomics. Every aspect of media has been impacted by idonomics, and the appeal to the lowest common denominator and pursuit of short-term profit at the expense of long-term commitment and quality. Broadcast television is a primetime example of the triumph of idonomics. While the 1980's were probably a highpoint for quality television shows, viewership and revenues, it has been a long slide to the bottom since then.

Scripted television shows – particularly comedies – have suffered a decline both in quality and quantity, with overall viewership declining dramatically. There are notable exceptions – terrific scripted dramatic and comedy shows that have become hits – but the past decade has been dominated by reality TV, which is cheap to make and appeals to a younger, raunchier aesthetic. Not that there is anything wrong with young and raunchy, but it does leave out the sensibilities of a large portion of the

American public. Ironically, it is cable television, which began as the low-budget stepchild to broadcast TV, that has produced much of the quality program over the last decade, but is also the source of a great deal of the sloppy sleaze that washes over the television sets of America.

Movies are another arena where idonomics runs rampant. Beginning in the 1980's with the success of movies by Spielberg, Coppola and other young directors, Hollywood discovered the "blockbuster." Believe it or not, the idea of a blockbuster movie that would make hundreds of millions of dollars had never been part of Hollywood's business plan. Since the 1930's, when there were a hundred million movie tickets sold every week – nearly ten times as many as today with half of the current population – Hollywood studios made lots and lots of movies. Some were flops, others were hits, but the studios didn't have to depend on a few movies to rack up huge profits. What's more, Hollywood focused on the domestic American market, which had most of the movie screens and represented most of the profits.

But with the arrival of television in the 1950's, the movie business went into a prolonged slump, which was only partially reversed by the blockbuster hits of the '70's and '80's. But from then on, Hollywood decided to place its big bets on blockbusters that would not only drive millions to the domestic box office, but also reap big rewards overseas, where more and more movie theaters were being built for a worldwide audience hungry for Hollywood-style movies. That was fine, but it isn't that easy to produce blockbuster movies year after year, especially when your main goal is to make lots of money and attract big audiences. Believe it or not, the generation of filmmakers like Spielberg, Lucas and Coppola began as outsider artists struggling against an entrenched studio system. Their goal was to make high-quality, innovative movies, not churn out blockbusters.

However, in true idonomics fashion, Hollywood transformed itself into a blockbuster machine. We all know the result. Year after year, and sequel after sequel, Hollywood spends millions producing and marketing films that are simply expensive copies of other films. Ticket sales have dropped off, and theater owners respond by raising prices. American audiences get bored with the films, so more and more movies are tailored to the international audience, which now represents more than sixty percent of movie revenues.

The result is action-oriented and special-effects movies with familiar movie stars that play well overseas but offer very little in terms of quality entertainment. Sure, Hollywood has always churned out cheap B-movies, but now we see nothing but expensive B-movies. The kind of middle-brow, family entertainment that Hollywood used to produce has simply migrated to cable television or independent cinemas.

It isn't only news, television and movies that have been affected by idonomics. The music business has also suffered, as music companies tried to squeeze short-term profits even as their sales were declining due to internet downloading. But it isn't new technology that is solely to blame for the decline of music business profits. From the beginnings of rock music, music companies have taken advantage of both performers and consumers, stripping out huge profits at the expense of building long-term relationships. When both performers and consumers decided they'd had enough of this idonomics deal, they bolted, leaving the music companies struggling to prop up an industry that had killed the goose that laid the golden egg.

Finally, the sports industry has also suffered from idonomics. While the economic impact of idonomics has not been as great on professional sports as in other areas of entertainment, it can be argued that the experience of sporting events has been devalued by idonomics, and may be threatened in the long run. Astronomical player salaries, rising ticket prices and lucrative television deals have made team owners even richer and sent the value of professional teams through the roof, but have the fans benefitted from the idonomics of sports? One can argue that the fans will ultimately reject the commercialization of America's pastimes and that the sports industry will also suffer as other entertainment fields have.

Like many other aspects of our lives, the world of entertainment has been severely impacted by idonomics. The pursuit of short-term profits means sacrificing quality art and entertainment, which require a long-term commitment to developing talent. Even in the old movie studio system, which was heavily criticized, the studio bosses knew that they had to put resources into nurturing the talent of the future, and that their investment would pay off in the long term. In the world of idonomics, there is no such thing as long-term commitment. Instant gratification rules their world.

The Idonomics of Technology

One might think that technology would be immune to the advent of idonomics. After all, technology is the result of scientific inquiry and discovery, and would seem to be above the pursuit of the pleasure principle. In fact, exactly the opposite is true. Let's examine, for example, where the major investments in new technology have been made in the past thirty years. Have we been investing in new technology to address the energy crisis? Not really. While there have been lots of promises to find technological solutions to our energy problem, there have been only modest investments in alternative energy technologies. How about new technologies to solve global environmental problems? Again, very modest investments. More efficient transportation like energy-efficient vehicles or mass transit? Nope. In fact, most of the efforts by auto makers and others have been fighting full efficiency standards.

Energy efficiency is not the only area that has suffered. Streamlining governmental efficiency, improving educational and infrastructure technology, increasing information access to the public and a host of other technology-related improvements have been neglected. Technology-based public communications have also lagged. While most nations now have widely available and affordable wireless network access, the United States remains in the very early stages of public wireless rollout. The lack of technology investment – or even a national technology policy – leaves us in a very weakened competitive position in the global marketplace.

There is lots of hype around the revolution in technology, and we see it everywhere in our daily lives. But where has the money been going? In true idonomics fashion, it has been going primarily into short-term corporate profits, speculative investment and new consumer devices. In short, the pursuit of pleasure over more productive deferred gratification. Certainly, there is no dispute that the advent of the personal computer, the internet and social networks has transformed the world, and generally for the better. However, the use of technology to meet an artificially created consumer demand has meant that many important uses of new technology have been neglected.

Can it really be argued that the latest version of the iPhone is as beneficial to the society as a nationwide public wireless network? Or that the rollout of the latest Facebook or Google feature is comparable to a modernization of our governmental technology infrastructure? While it is true that Facebook and Google – along with a host of other technology companies and innovations – have brought us billions in revenues and millions of new jobs, does that mean that other, less profitable technology innovations should be ignored?

A simple analogy is the plight of the homeowner with a leaky roof. While she might want to spend her limited funds on a 3D television set to replace her three-year old digital version, does that really make sense when her roof is leaking every time it rains? A spending plan that balances prudent investment in home maintenance, savings and insurance protection with other, perhaps more entertaining items like TVs, video games and computers is the most sensible course. However, as a society, we are spending most of our technology money on consumer products while the rain is leaking into our house. Idonomics in action.

Lord, Won't You Buy Me a Mercedes Benz

In a famous song from the 1960's, Janis Joplin plaintively asks God to buy her a luxury car, along with a few other items from her wish list. While people have often pleaded with the deity for health, wealth and happiness, idonomics have changed the face of religion over the past thirty years. Throughout American history, revivalist preachers in the Bible belt would set up tents to preach to the faithful, practice miracle cures and pass the hat to collect money for their spiritual mission. However, with the advent of televangelists who used satellite broadcasts to reach millions of viewers, the ritual "passing the hat" was transformed into a mega-marketing campaign that reaped millions for the popular televangelists.

And what was it that the televangelists were preaching? In addition to the solace of faith that traditional Christianity had offered, the televangelists seemed to be promising a lot more. Faith in God and prayers to Jesus could deliver earthly rewards, they suggested, in the form of wealth, personal happiness, better health and loving relationships. While traditional churches never denied that believing in God might be beneficial and that living a good Christian life had its rewards – both on earth and in heaven, most did not go as far as the televangelists in offering immediate material benefits in our daily lives.

In this way, the televangelists had more in common with practitioners of the popular self-help movements that arose in the 1980's than with traditional religion. Televangelists urged their flock to rely on faith and prayer to solve everything from unemployment to marital difficulties and alcoholism. Everything from the start a new business venture to saving a marriage could somehow be improved by heeding the televangelists' call to faith – along with a generous donation to televangelists' churches. Critics labeled the televangelists as hucksters, while true believers called them messengers of God. Whatever you call them, they were practicing idonomics to the hilt.

It is hard to make the case that asking God for wealth, health or personal happiness will make it happen. While there are undoubtedly many cases where faith and prayer made a material difference in people's everyday lives, there are certainly many more cases where the fervent wish was not fulfilled. Whatever your view of this brand of religion, it appears to rest largely on a desire for immediate gratification -- in short, the desire to gain pleasure and avoid pain. Does that sound familiar? It is the very definition of the pleasure principle and the essential dynamic of idonomics.

Religions have long struggled with the issue of personal intervention by the deity, and there a vast theoretical tracts that argue all sides of the debate, which will certainly not be settled here. What is clear, however, is that in the past thirty years, with the rise of televangelism and the decline of traditional religion, that idonomics has deeply affected the practice of religion in the United States. The infusion of politics into religious activity is simply another sign of the rise of religious idonomics. Instead of focusing on the mystery of faith and our personal connection with God, the practitioners of religious idonomics are espousing political doctrines as both easy fixes to complex social problems and as articles of religious faith. This is certainly a distortion of the role of religion both in American political life and in the religious life of our citizens.

Cultural Idonomics

It should be no surprise that the rise of idonomics in the past thirty years has greatly affected our cultural values and mores. While Americans have always prided themselves on their individuality and love of personal freedom, there has also been a traditional strain of self-sacrifice and dedication to the greater community. From the Boy Scout helping the senior citizen across the street to young men and women volunteering to serve in the military, America has been built on a sense of responsibility, respect and a concern for others. However, if you look around at America today, you see a decline in many of those time-honored values.

How often do you see a young man to offer his seat on the bus to an old lady or pregnant woman? What about the guy chatting loudly on his cell phone in the middle of the supermarket? Or the young woman giving the middle finger salute to the driver of a slow-moving vehicle? While these may seem like small matters, they are indicative of a much bigger trend in our society – the arrival of cultural idonomics.

Simply put, cultural idonomics are based on the principle of "me first." Whether it is road rage on the highways or the selfish behavior of celebrities, the cultural premise is tilting toward the prerogatives of the individual over the welfare of the group. Beginning with the cultural revolution of the 1960's against authority and authority figures, traditional notions of courtesy and politeness came to be viewed as outdated and stuffy. In the same way, the rebellion against the American puritanical tradition opened the floodgates for in-your-face sexuality in the form of pornography, commercialization of sex and objectification of women. This developed to an extreme where women were routinely referred to as prostitutes and men as pimps in popular media.

And it's not only in the worlds of media and entertainment where traditional values have been replaced with rampant, over-the-top idonomics. Our political debate has descended into vicious name-calling and even threats, to the extent that a sitting Congressman shouted out that the President was a liar during the State of the Union address. Any vestige of restraint or impulse control has clearly gone out the window. In virtually every profession and trade, a sense of ethics seems to have been sorely tested, if not completely abandoned. Bankers, mortgage brokers, investment advisors and stock brokers routinely bend or break both ethical and legal rules in their pursuit of the bottom line. Government officials and corporate executives routinely lie or "spin" the truth and get away with it, because average citizens believe that "everybody does it."

The view that "everybody does it" is a pernicious byproduct of idonomics. At its heart, idonomics dictates that everyone is out for themselves, with little regard for the common welfare. Why should I pay my taxes, they ask, when the guy down the street, or the rich guy uptown, is not paying his? Why should I support the schools when I don't have any kids? Why should I conserve energy when my neighbor leaves his lights on all the time? The road of idonomics is a slippery slope down the path of social Darwinism, where only the fittest survive, and the nation as a whole suffers.

There are hundreds of cultural and social issues – from abortion and gun control to welfare and pornography – about which citizens can disagree. But when the cultural values revolve simply around "me first" – and the hell with everybody else – we are on a path to social discord and destruction. By embracing cultural idonomics, we endanger some of our most precious cultural values, which focus on common sense, self-sacrifice and concern for others.

Relationship Idonomics

It is easy to understand how idonomics has profoundly affected economics, media, politics, technology, and even our religious and cultural values, but has it really reached into our personal relationships with family and friends? The answer, unfortunately, is that it has. Since the 1980's, the divorce rate has tripled in most Western countries, including the United States. While it can be argued that greater independence for women and changing economic conditions have been partly responsible for the skyrocketing divorce rate, it is also clear that idonomics plays an important role in these statistics.

With a greater societal emphasis on individual freedom and the pursuit of the pleasure principle, it is little wonder that many couples decide to abandon the responsibilities of marriage – and sometimes even parenthood. When there is less stigma placed on divorce and more focus on immediate gratification, the temptations to stray from the challenges and vicissitudes of marriage are great. Although there has always been a tension between the strictures of monogamy and the temptation to wander, idonomics has tilted the balance in favor of wandering.

Successful marriages – as well as parenting and friendships – require constant compromise, the give-and-take that makes human relationships both challenging and dynamic. Every successful marriage requires a deep commitment to stick with the partnership through good times and bad, since there are usually plenty of both. Marriage, along with parenthood and strong friendships, requires hard work and an investment in the future of the relationship. In short, these relationships require deferred gratification and self-sacrifice, both of which have no place in idonomics.

Another important challenge to modern relationships is the rise in alcoholism and drug abuse. While alcohol and drug addiction have long been a part of our society, the easy availability of drugs and alcohol, along with the declining stigma attached to addiction, have led to a dramatic rise in the rates of addiction. More than twenty million Americans use illegal drugs, and hospital admissions due to drug use have doubled in the past thirty years. At the same time, more than fifteen million Americans are dependent on alcohol, which can have a dramatic impact on American families.

Family dysfunction can also result in serious domestic violence and abuse. Domestic violence is the leading cause of injury to women—more than car accidents, muggings, and rapes combined. It is estimated that nearly ten million children have witnessed instances of domestic violence. While domestic violence has always been a grave social concern, the rise of domestic violence can be tracked to the "me first" credo of idonomcs and the lack of social strictures that call for respect for others.

Overcoming Idonomics

Over the past thirty years, idonomics has dominated our economic, political and personal lives, impacting everything from media and entertainment to religion and marriage. Idonomics has damaged our economy, undermined our cultural and spiritual values, threatened our health and our relationships and jeopardized the American dream. After the calamity of the Great Recession – the ultimate consequence of idonomics – the question is how we can overcome the scourge of idonomics.

Unfortunately, it is not as easy to undo the damage of idonomics as it was to skip down that primrose path in the first place. Willpower alone – just saying "no" to the pursuit of pleasure – certainly won't work. Deferred gratification – which is the only way to fight idonomics – is a complicated and challenging process, as research studies over the past fifty years have shown us. But there are hopeful signs that we can overcome the power of idonomics and follow a more realistic path in our lives and our world.

Remember Walter Mischel and his "marshmallow" experiments? One of his key findings was that two-thirds of the four-year olds in the experiment were not able to resist the impulse to quickly eat the marshmallow in front of them, even if waiting meant a bigger treat later. However, one-third of the children were able to defer gratification for a later reward. Interestingly enough, follow-up studies of the children who deferred gratification showed that they performed better on everything from SAT scores to personal relationships later in life. But what about the other two-thirds? What explained their inability to defer gratification?

Subsequent research by Mischel and others focused on wide range of factors from socioeconomic and cultural background to personality traits. None of these studies produced significant differences in "delaying" or "non-delaying" behavior. Perhaps the "non-delayers" simply wanted the marshmallows more? No, studies revealed that both groups really wanted the treat. Mischel concluded that neither nature nor nurture could explain – or predict – who would be more successful at deferring gratification. While it seemed that their ability to defer gratification had some genetic origins, they remained a mystery.

So the researchers took another tack. Would it be possible, they asked, for the "non-delayers" to learn delayed gratification? And, if so, how could they learn it? Research studies began to focus on how "delayers" were able to defer gratification. What were the techniques that they used to avoid temptation? The results were startlingly clear. The four-year olds used what came to be called "strategic allocation of attention." That meant avoiding focusing on the marshmallows by covering their eyes, hiding under the desk or singing songs.

Scientists refer to this technique as "metacognition" or "thinking about thinking" which allowed the children to overcome the temptation of the marshmallow. We all develop important "rules of thinking." In this case, not looking at or thinking about the marshmallow was a way to avoid eating it. While the "delayers" used this technique to avoid thinking about the marshmallow, the "non-delayers" decided the best strategy was to focus intently on the goal – staring at the marshmallow instead of hiding their eyes. They had the rules backwards, and as a result, rarely were able to defer gratification for very long.

Research continues on these distraction techniques for delayed gratification. However, there seem to be two general principles at work that offer promise for promoting delayed gratification. First is the use of mental tricks such as imagining the marshmallow is a picture rather than an actual piece of candy, or envisioning a cloud or a flower in place of the marshmallow. The second, and perhaps more promising approach is "peer modeling." Preliminary studies of kindergarteners who were shown a video of a child using delayed gratification techniques improved significantly in delaying gratification.

Of course, it is a long journey from teaching young children ways to delay gratification to overcoming the social and cultural underpinnings of idonomics. However, the Great Recession and a new appreciation of risk and uncertainty have provided a powerful opportunity for our society to change course. Profound lessons about risk and the unbridled pursuit of pleasure often make a lasting imprint. But we must be continually reminded of those lessons, which we have a tendency to easily forget.

Reclaiming the American Dream

America and the American Dream have always occupied a unique place in the world. Throughout our history, we have been seen around the globe as a land of promise and opportunity. We are an immigrant nation where millions have settled, seeking greater freedom for themselves and a better future for their children. Over the past thirty years, the American Dream has been put in jeopardy by idonomics and the unrestrained pursuit of the pleasure principle.

Few would argue that we need to embrace a new Puritanism or extreme form of self-sacrifice. For most of our history, Americans have practiced a common-sense approach to everything from economics and politics to religion and community responsibility. There is no reason to shackle ourselves to strict frugality or self-denial any more than we should continue on the destructive path of idonomics. What we need to do as a society – using some of the techniques of delayed gratification that we have discussed – is take a reality-based approach to all areas of our lives, and resist the temptation to act impulsively.

Economists – and their newly arrived brethren, neuroeconomists – have exhaustively studied human behavior in the economic and social realms, and have provided useful guides for us as society to pursue reality-based decision making. While no one would argue that we should become a hyper-conservative or risk-averse society, there is certainly an opportunity for abandoning idonomics after our experience of the Great Recession.

It also is worth noting that other countries have problems quite different than the American brand of idonomics. While many Western countries have succumbed to a global exuberance for idonomics, others have barely been affected. China and Japan, for example, have the opposite problem. Their citizens save too much, practically hoarding their money and thereby retarding investment and growth of their economies. But for those of us in America and the West, we could use a dose of their Asian frugality.

Can the American Dream survive idonomics? Absolutely. By applying traditional American values of common sense and practicality with newer research techniques for promoting deferred gratification, we can certainly get back on the right path. While nobody wants to turn back the clock or return to the hardscrabble days of the Great Depression, we can embrace a new vision of the American Dream that will provide opportunity and freedom for all Americans. If we think of idonomics as the feverish frenzy of the past, and begin to build our economy, our government and religious institutions, our media and communications, and even our families and community on a more solid, practical foundation, we can overcome the excesses of the past and return the American Dream to its rightful place.

ABOUT THE AUTHOR

Hoyt Hilsman

Hoyt Hilsman is an award-winning writer, critic and former candidate for Congress in California. He has written screenplays for the major film studios and television networks, as well as hundreds of articles for national newspapers and magazines, including *The New York Times, The Los Angeles Times, Hemispheres* and *The National Law Journal*. A former critic for *Variety*, he is now a regular contributor to *The Huffington Post*, and was a recipient of the Apex Award for Excellence in Journalism. His novel, *19 Angels*, a political thriller set in the Middle East, was published in 2011.

Hoyt grew up in Washington, DC, where his father was an advisor to President Kennedy. He has been active politics and public policy, working with various national figures, including Bill Clinton, an as an advisor to several campaigns. He has been a director at the Hope Street Group and a member of the Pacific Council on International Policy, as well as a consultant to a number of corporations, universities, non-profits and government organizations, including The Kennedy Space Center, Idealab! and others.

For more info, please visit www.hoythilsman.com